This book is to be returned on or before the last date stamped below or you will be charged a fine

New City College – Tower Hamlets
Learning Resource Centre
Poplar High Street
London E14 0AF
http://library.tower.ac.uk
Poplar: 020 7510 7765   **Arbour Sq**: 020 7510 7568

Or you can visit our Inter

attention of the publisher and verified to the satisfaction of the publisher will be corrected in future editions.

ISBN 0-7876-6942-3
ISSN 1094-3552

Printed in the United States of America
10 9 8 7 6 5 4 3 2 1

Wide Sargasso Sea

Jean Rhys

1966

Introduction

Wide Sargasso Sea, published in 1966 toward the end of Jean Rhys's writing career, was the most successful of Rhys's literary works. The novel was well received when it was first published and has never been out of print. It also continues to draw the interest of academics and literary critics today. The popularity of *Wide Sargasso Sea* might be based on several factors. The general reader might enjoy this novel for the captivating story of a lonely young woman who is driven to near madness by her need to be loved. Literary theorists, on the other hand, find Rhys's novel rich in the portrayal of the damaging effects of colonization on a conquered people and the debilitating consequences of sexual exploitation of women. Another group of readers, those interested in multiculturalism, might be drawn to *Wide Sargasso Sea* for the insider's view that Rhys provides of nineteenth-century life and culture on a Caribbean island.

Wide Sargasso Sea was written as Rhys's attempt to explain the character of Bertha Mason in Charlotte Brontë's *Jane Eyre*. Rhys wanted to explore the reasons why Bertha Mason went mad. In doing so, Rhys fills her story with conflict. There is the clash between former slaves and their previous owners; the overall misunderstandings between the white and black races; the disparity in beliefs between the old white plantation owners and the new English immigrants who come to live on the island. There is also the battle between men and women as they try to satisfy their needs through their relationships with one another. And finally, the ultimate conflict, the interior confusion the protagonist must face between her emotional and rational state of being.

Wide Sargasso Sea was honored with the prestigious W. H. Smith Award and the Heinemann Award of the Royal Society of Literature. The novel was also selected by Random House as one of the best one hundred books of fiction written in the English language during the twentieth century.

Author Biography

Jean Rhys was born in Roseau, Dominica, on August 24, 1890. Her father was a Welsh doctor. When she was sixteen years old, she was sent to England to live with an aunt and to attend the Perse School at Cambridge and later the Royal Academy of Dramatic Art. Although Dominica would influence her writing, Rhys would return to her birthplace only once, in 1936. When her father died, Rhys was forced to take on a variety of jobs in England, which included working as a chorus girl with a touring musical company, a mannequin, an artist's model, and a ghostwriter of a book about furniture.

In 1919, she moved to Paris with her husband, Jean Lenglet, a French-Dutch journalist and song-writer. In the same year, she gave birth to a son, who died when he was three weeks old. She later had a daughter. Around this same time, Rhys met Ford Madox Ford, with whom she had an affair while her husband was in jail for illegal financial transactions. Ford encouraged Rhys's writing and also wrote the introduction for Rhys's first book *The Left Bank* (1927), a collection of short stories. Rhys's marriage to Lenglet ended in divorce. Rhys would marry twice again. Each of these marriages left her a widow.

Rhys's first novel, published in the States as *Quartet* (1929) (originally published as *Postures* in

Britain), was supposedly based on Rhys's affair with Ford. It was in this work that Rhys's sensitive, sexually attractive, vulnerable, and somewhat self-defeating heroine is first introduced, a figure that is often repeated in Rhys's later books. Subsequent works include *After Leaving Mr. Mackenzie* (1930); *Voyage in the Dark* (1934), reportedly Rhys's most autobiographical work; and *Good Morning Midnight* (1939).

For the next twenty years or so, Rhys disappeared from public view. Many people thought she had died. Then in 1958, Britain's BBC produced a drama based on Rhys's *Good Morning Midnight*. In 1966, her *Wide Sargasso Sea* was published to critical acclaim.

Rhys did not receive much critical acclaim for her works during most of her lifetime, and when it finally arrived in her later years, Rhys stated that it came too late. Contemporary critics studying her work today believe that the reason for Rhys's going virtually unnoticed in the literary world was that she was ahead of her time. Feminist theorists, in particular, believe that Rhys's theme of women as exploited victims was not easily accepted in Rhys's day. After the publication of *Wide Sargasso Sea*, however, Rhys was made a CBE (Commander of the order of the British Empire, an honor bestowed by the queen) in 1978. She was also awarded the W. H. Smith Award for her last novel, as well as the Royal Society of Literature Award and an Arts Council Bursary. She died on May 14, 1979, in Exeter. Her unfinished autobiography was published posthumously under the title *Smile Please* (1979).

Plot Summary

Part 1

The first part of *Wide Sargasso Sea* is narrated by the female protagonist, Antoinette. She explains that she lives in isolation from the rest of the population of the small Caribbean island on which her family's plantation exists. The story opens in 1839 after the recent emancipation of slaves in the British Empire. The emancipation has not only caused her family to live in poverty but also to have to face the tension of freed slaves, as both the white and the black citizens of the island sort through their new relationships.

The picture that Rhys paints in part 1 is that of isolation. Of the main characters, Antoinette appears to feel the effects of that isolation the most. She lives with her mother, Annette Cosway, and her brother, Pierre, who suffers from some unnamed mental disability. Antoinette's mother spends most of her time mothering Pierre, at Antoinette's expense. Antoinette is forced to look for affection in other places. She tries to befriend the young black children who live in the nearby countryside, but she is made fun of and even threatened. So she turns to Christophine, the woman who cooks for the family and becomes a mother figure for Antoinette. Without Christophine, Antoinette says the family would have died. Christophine introduces

Antoinette to the child of a friend. The girl's name is Tia. Antoinette and Tia spend several days together, swimming and eating. But one day, Antoinette becomes angry with Tia and calls her a "nigger." It is a name she herself had been called in the past: a "white nigger." The two young girls argue, and the friendship ends.

Around this same time, Antoinette's mother makes friends with a new family of white people, whom Christophine refers to as "[t]rouble." Antoinette's mother sells the last of her jewelry to buy material to make dresses for herself and Antoinette, to make themselves presentable. And shortly afterward, Antoinette's mother marries Mr. Mason.

With Mason's money, the family estate, Coulibri, is refurbished. However, Mason is careless in his attitude toward the black servants, and Antoinette's mother becomes filled with fear that something awful will happen. Antoinette, however, feels safe. Coulibri is the only place she feels secure. Fortune does not shine on the family, however. The local black people do not like Mr. Mason, and one night they burn down the family home. As the family attempts to escape, an angry mob awaits them outside. Only when the angry blacks see the Mason family parrot, with his feathers caught on fire, attempt to fly over their heads, do the blacks disperse. The burning parrot represents an evil omen to them. As the family makes its escape, Antoinette sees Tia and starts to run to her, believing that they are still friends. But

Tia hurls a rock at Antoinette, which hits her on the head and knocks her unconscious. When Antoinette later awakens from a long illness, she discovers that her brother, Pierre, has died and her mother has been taken away. Antoinette is now living with her Aunt Cora. This section ends with a description of Antoinette's experiences at a convent school.

Part 2

The beginning of the second part of the story is narrated by the man who has married Antoinette. He remains unnamed throughout the story. However, since it has been acknowledged that Rhys has written *Wide Sargasso Sea* as a prequel to Brontë's *Jane Eyre* and because the details she offers about the male narrator match Brontë's male protagonist, it is easily assumed that this is Brontë's Edward Rochester.

Antoinette has left the convent school and has married Rochester. This marriage was arranged by Antoinette's stepbrother, Richard Mason. Antoinette cannot gain her inheritance unless she agrees to marry a man of Mason's choice. Rochester, the younger son of a British gentleman, has come to Jamaica for this precise reason.

Media Adaptations

- John Duigan directed a movie of *Wide Sargasso Sea* (1993). It starred Karina Lombard as Antoinette, Michael York as her father, Rachel Ward as her mother, Nathaniel Parker as her husband, and Claudia Robinson as Christophine. Although some critics believe that sexuality was favored over character development, the movie provides a relatively honest portrayal of two deteriorating marriages. It is currently available on DVD. Jan Louter, fascinated by the novel, made a documentary film about Rhys and her world in the Caribbean.

The newlyweds have returned to the "little estate in the Windward Islands," as Rochester describes it in a letter to his father. The place is Ganbois, property that Antoinette has inherited. Rochester is recovering from an illness, and he finds everything about the island too intense, from the colors of the landscape to the scent that Antoinette puts in her hair. Rochester does, however, promise Antoinette "peace, happiness, [and] safety," none of which he is ultimately able to give her. He is rather depressed about his marriage, wondering if he has sold his soul for money.

Forever swayed by doubt about his marriage and his wife, Rochester is easily influenced by a mysterious letter he receives from Daniel Cosway, who claims to be Antoinette's half brother. Cosway tells Rochester about Antoinette's mother's instability and suggests that Antoinette is not a virgin. In fact, Cosway names Antoinette's previous sexual partner as Sandi Cosway, her black cousin. Although prior to this letter Rochester seems to be trying to create a relationship with Antoinette, he now wants nothing to do with her. Rochester's narration ends with him reading a book about voodoo.

Antoinette now takes up the narration. She is miserable because Rochester will have nothing to do with her. She goes to Christophine and asks for a potion that will make Rochester want to make love to her. Although Christophine protests that "if the man don't love you, I can't make him love you," she gives Antoinette what she has asked for.

Rochester receives another note from Daniel, who demands that Rochester visit him, which he does. Daniel claims to be the illegitimate son of "old Cosway." Daniel is angry because Cosway never acknowledged him. Daniel also gives Rochester more details about Antoinette's affair with Sandi. When Rochester returns home, he questions Antoinette briefly but won't let her complete all her thoughts. She insists and fills him in on some of her background. In the midst of her telling, Rochester refers to Antoinette as Bertha, another reference to Brontë's *Jane Eyre*. Bertha, in Brontë's novel, was the mad woman who lived in the attic, Rochester's first wife.

The next morning, Rochester feels sick and recalls very little of what happened the previous night. He thinks he might have been poisoned. Later, when he is feeling better, he makes love to Amelie, a servant girl who comes with food to his room. When Antoinette confronts Rochester about his sexual encounter with Amelie, he confesses that he does not love Antoinette.

Christophine tries to help Antoinette, who is totally distraught. Rochester confronts Christophine and tells her to leave. Christophine does her best to stand up for Antoinette, asking Rochester to give back at least half of the money so Antoinette can have a new start on life. She tells him to leave Antoinette with her. But Rochester is a confused man. He looks for a sign that Antoinette loves him, but he does not find it. So he packs up all their belongings and plans to sell the house. He refers to

Antoinette as his "lunatic," and he is taking her to England.

Part 3

Part three begins with a new narrator, Grace Poole, another character from Brontë's novel. Poole has been hired to take care of Antoinette. Rochester's father and brother have died, making Rochester a very rich man. He is not at the English estate but rather he is traveling. Grace finds Rochester's home "safe," and she accepts the job. Then the narration is turned over to Antoinette.

Antoinette's mind is obviously caught between dream and reality. She mixes memories up with the present time, so it is not clear what is really happening and what she is imagining. However, she mentions having made love to her cousin Sandi. And she talks about how cold and isolated she is, living in the attic of Rochester's estate. She talks about setting the house on fire and then wanders back to her memories of Coulibri in flames. As this short section of the story comes to an end, Antoinette takes a burning candle in hand. "Now at last I know why I was brought here and what I have to do," she says.

Characters

Amelie

Amelie is a servant girl at Ganbois, the house to which Rochester and Antoinette go after they are married. Rochester comments that Amelie reminds him of Antoinette. The day after Antoinette has secretly slipped a potion into his wine, Rochester has sex with Amelie. He then gives Amelie money so she can leave the island.

Baptiste

Baptiste is a manservant at Ganbois. Although not overtly supportive of Antoinette, he does sympathize with her, especially when Rochester forces Antoinette to leave Ganbois.

Bertha

Several times, Rochester refers to Antoinette as Bertha. He tells her that he likes that name and likes to think of her as Bertha. This is Rhys's reference to Brontë's story in which Bertha is Rochester's first wife.

Aunt Cora

Aunt Cora takes Antoinette into her home

when Antoinette's mother is taken away. Aunt Cora does not approve of Antoinette's stepfather, Mr. Mason, nor of his son, Richard Mason. She also does not like the suitor Richard has arranged to marry Antoinette, Edward Rochester. Aunt Cora takes care of Antoinette after Coulibri burns down and Antoinette is knocked unconscious.

Annette Cosway

Annette Cosway is Antoinette's mother. Her first husband is dead when the story opens and Annette is depressed. She and her family are living in near poverty. She is the mother of two children and has little means of raising them. She leaves Antoinette on her own for most of the time. When she meets a group of rich people who befriend her, she eagerly jumps at the chance to be wed to Mr. Mason. She finds little happiness in her marriage, and with the destruction of Coulibri and the death of her son, she withdraws from reality.

Antoinette Cosway

The character of Antoinette is based on Charlotte Brontë's Bertha Mason in *Jane Eyre*. Bertha is the first wife of Brontë's protagonist Edward Rochester. In Brontë's story, Rochester kept Bertha locked up in the attic. Rhys wanted to tell the story from Bertha's point of view. So Antoinette is the younger version of Bertha, before she moved to England with her husband. Rhys's story demonstrates how Antoinette goes "mad."

Antoinette, the female protagonist, is a very young girl at the beginning of the story. Her childhood is difficult and marks her personality. Her father is dead. Her brother's dependence on her mother deprives Antoinette of motherly affection, and she is left to fend for herself. Her greatest support comes from Christophine, the woman who cooks for the family. Otherwise, Antoinette is very much on her own and is often lonely and scared.

Antoinette cannot find any place to fit in, except when she is alone. She is not as "white" as the well-to-do white plantation owners. She is also not as "black" as the freed slaves. Having Creole ancestors from the island of Martinique, she is considered an island outsider in Jamaica and Dominica. The closest she comes to a sense of security is while she is alone at Coulibri, which is burnt to the ground when she is still young. Later, when she returns to the property, she accuses her husband of further destroying her security by cursing her family home with his bitterness and the great sadness he has caused her.

Although she has fallen helplessly in love with her husband, it is an unrequited love. Rochester's unfaithfulness tortures her further, and finally she, like her mother, withdraws into a world of her own.

Daniel Cosway

Daniel is the person who writes a letter to Rochester, telling him about the instability of Antoinette's mother and of Antoinette's supposed sexual encounter before she met Rochester. Daniel claims to be Antoinette's illegitimate half brother. Because of Daniel's accusations, Rochester becomes confused about his feelings for his wife and later decides that Antoinette is a "lunatic."

Pierre Cosway

Pierre is Antoinette's brother. He has a mental deficiency, but his specific problem is never disclosed. Antoinette's mother provides Pierre with constant care, while disallowing Antoinette any affection. When Coulibri is burnt, Pierre suffers and dies.

Sandi Cosway

Sandi is a distant cousin of Antoinette. He protects her in a brief scene when Antoinette is walking to school. Later, rumors are stirred about Antoinette and Sandi having been lovers, before Antoinette is married. Her liaison with Sandi, after Rochester forces Antoinette to leave Ganbois, enrages Rochester and is the stimulus for Rochester taking Antoinette to England. At the end of the book, Antoinette enjoys her memories of Sandi's last kiss. It may be the closest she ever comes to love.

Christophine Dubois

Christophine is a servant at Coulibri. She is also Antoinette's closest confidant. Her reputation as an obeah, or practitioner of voodoo, causes some people to fear her. Antoinette does not fear Christophine and often goes to her for counsel. Christophine is a mother figure for Antoinette, someone who notices her loneliness and tries to mend it. Christophine also admonishes Antoinette's mother for her lack of affection and care toward her daughter.

After she is married and her husband loses his desire for her, Antoinette asks Christophine to make a potion so her husband will love her and want her again. Christophine is wary of using voodoo in this way. When the potion fails, Christophine is the only person who understands the effects of Antoinette's broken heart, and she tries to help Antoinette, once again. Rochester finally sends Christophine away, threatening to turn her over to the police for her illegal voodoo practice.

Mr. Luttrell

Mr. Luttrell is the only friend that Antoinette's mother has in the space of time between her husband's death and her marrying Mr. Mason. Luttrell lived on the plantation next to Coulibri and one day "swam out to sea and was gone for always." He represents one of the old white families who suffered economically after the emancipation of slaves.

Mannie

Mannie is a manservant at Coulibri. He is one of the few black people who is loyal to Antoinette's family and who tries to extinguish the fire that destroys the house.

Annette Mason

See Annette Cosway

Mr. Mason

Mr. Mason (no first name is ever provided) is Antoinette's stepfather, the man whom her mother marries in the first part of the story. Mason has money but lacks affection, especially for the freed slaves. He does, however, use his money to refurbish Coulibri. Ironically, it is mostly due to his de-meaning attitude toward the black community that the freed slaves rise against the family and burn the house to the ground. This and his lack of affection drive his wife mad. In his own way, he cares about Antoinette's future and tries to arrange a marriage for her before his death.

Richard Mason

Richard is Mr. Mason's son. It is Richard who brings Rochester to the islands and sees to the details of Antoinette's marriage to Rochester. His appearances in the story are brief, but he is partially responsible for setting Antoinette onto the path to madness. He gives Rochester the power over all of Antoinette's inheritance and thus the power over her life. He reappears at the end of the story, visiting Antoinette in England. She attacks him with a knife.

Myra

Myra is a servant at Coulibri. It is suggested that Myra reports all of Mr. Mason's derogatory comments to the other black people in the community. Myra is supposed to be taking care of Antoinette's brother on the night of the fire. She mysteriously disappears just as the flames begin in the brother's room.

Grace Poole

Grace narrates the first section of part 3. She has been hired to take care of Antoinette in England. She, like Antoinette, feels that the outside world is dangerous. She feels safe in the big house, and she receives extra money for taking special care of Antoinette, who sometimes frightens her.

Edward Rochester

Although he is never named in *Wide Sargasso Sea*, the male protagonist of this story is derived from *Jane Eyre*'s Edward Rochester. He is Antoinette's husband, and he narrates most of the second part of the story. Rochester comes to the islands in search of wealth but later feels he has sold his soul when he finds his money in Antoinette's inheritance. He is the second son of an English gentleman and therefore not entitled to an inheritance of his own. He is also somewhat sickly and weak of spirit and is easily persuaded that he has been deceived. The islands are very exotic to him and not in a way that he find pleasant. He completely misreads Antoinette's needs and her love and concludes that she is a "lunatic."

At first he is taken by her, at least on a physical level. It does not take long, however, for him to be repulsed by her scent and touch. When Antoinette tries to use a love potion on him, he seeks revenge by making love to one of the servants, within hearing distance of Antoinette. This truly drives her mad. He further punishes her by taking her away from her beloved family estate. Then, when he learns of a possible affair she has with a distant cousin, he forces her to go to England with him, where he locks her away in the attic. Although Antoinette's personality is never stable, it is Rochester who pushes her over the edge.

Tia

Tia is the closest that Antoinette comes to having a childhood friend. She is the daughter of one of Christophine's friends. Christophine introduces Antoinette to Tia in hopes that the relationship might cure some of Antoinette's loneliness. For a while, Tia and Antoinette are friends, swimming together and sharing their food. One day, when Tia tricks Antoinette out of a few pennies, Antoinette refers to Tia as a "nigger." This angers Tia, and she puts on Antoinette's dress after swimming, instead of her own. The two children do not see one another until the night of the fire at Coulibri. Antoinette runs to Tia, hoping to embrace her. Tia, however, throws a rock and hits Antoinette on the head, knocking her out. Although they never see one another again, Antoinette imagines, at the end of the story as she is preparing to burn down Rochester's house in England, that Tia is waiting for her when it is all done.

Isolation

Antoinette lives on a small island throughout most of this novel. The island itself represents the sense of isolation that overwhelms Antoinette throughout this story. In the beginning of the story, Antoinette and her mother and brother live far away from even the small island towns. Furthering their isolation is the fact that her mother is from another island, thus making them, in the eyes of the local people, outsiders. But it is not just the island people who isolate Antoinette's family. The other white landowners, many of them recent immigrants, have little to do with Antoinette's family because they are extremely poor. And although a handful of former slaves remain faithful to the family, most of the black people who live around them want nothing to do with them and eventually force Antoinette's family to leave by burning down their home.

In many ways, Antoinette's feelings of isolation are mirrored in her mother. Annette Cosway is a widow trying to raise two children on her own. She has the extra burden of caring for a son who suffers from a mental disability. Annette is a woman who needs to be loved but who cannot find it. She is accused of using her sexuality, however, to find a second husband, one who has sufficient money to help take care of her family. Mr.

Mason is not capable of love, however, so Annette withdraws further into herself. When her son is burned to death, her final link to reality is snapped, and she collapses into the dark isolation of her own inner world.

Antoinette also is starved for love. She tries to befriend the children her own age, but is turned away because she is white and they are black. Except for one brief encounter with Tia, a young black girl, Antoinette has no childhood friends. Antoinette is further isolated because her mother is consumed with two major challenges of her own: taking care of her disabled son and searching for love, or at least searching for someone who will help ease her financial burdens. Without the reassuring love of a mother, Antoinette finds herself living in a world that is dominated only by her own thoughts, fears, and needs.

When Antoinette is forced to live with her Aunt Cora, she is isolated in different ways. First, she is not allowed to see her mother. Then, the school that she attends is run by nuns who live behind tall, gated walls. This isolates Antoinette from the local children, who often threaten her. Antoinette is also unable to return to her childhood sanctuary, that of her family's estate. She has been cut off from the only place that she had previously known.

After Antoinette marries, her sense of isolation is momentarily relieved. She has found love and is returned to the land that she loves. However, this period is short-lived, as she soon discovers that her husband does not love her. When he makes love to another woman, even the relief of living on her ancestral land is stolen from her. The estate now makes Antoinette feel only unhappiness, and she begins to withdraw further into herself. By the end of the novel, Antoinette lives in an attic room in a large house in England. Now she finds herself in a completely foreign setting, one that is cold and dark. She no longer has the vibrant colors and the warmth of her island home. Her mother, brother, and father are dead. She has been removed from her aunt and from the mother figure of Christophine. Her husband stays completely away from her. Her only companion is a hired caretaker. It is here that Antoinette falls into the deepest isolation from the world. She is so far removed that she lives halfway between dream and reality.

Hunger

There are many different representations of hunger throughout this story. The story opens with Antoinette and her family living in poverty. So there is the obvious physical hunger caused by lack of food. But there is also the hunger for affection. Both mother and daughter, Annette and Antoinette, search for love. The mother tries to find that love in a man, whereas Antoinette looks for love from her mother. Later, Antoinette searches for affection from a friend, in the form of Tia. When Antoinette marries, her hungers are satisfied momentarily. The hunger for love, as well as for sexual expression, appears to be somewhat soothed. But this does not last long. As a matter of fact, in having felt love for the first time, when it is taken away from her, the hunger becomes even stronger. Her hunger to be loved eventually drives her mad.

Other hungers include the hunger for money, such as Rochester's, which makes him sell his soul in marrying Antoinette for her inheritance. There is also the hunger for land as white immigrants move to the island and establish large plantations on which to make a living. There is the hunger for freedom as ex-slaves fight for their rights and establish a new way of life. A hunger to be understood is played out between Antoinette and her husband, as mistrust builds between them. And on a more subtle level, there is Antoinette's hunger to feel safe, which is never fully realized.

Madness

Both Antoinette and her mother suffer mental breakdowns. They withdraw into their own private worlds, places deep inside of them where they are consumed by their thoughts so completely that they cannot distinguish between their fantasies and reality. They are forced there as a retreat from the circumstances of their lives. Annette's final link with reality is shattered when Coulibri burns down and her son dies. Antoinette's descent may have begun when she was a child, but it is the disintegration of her marriage and the move to England that finalize her fate. As Rhys presents it, both mother and daughter might have been saved from their collapse into madness had they received the affection and understanding that they so desperately needed.

Topics for Further Study

- *Wide Sargasso Sea* was inspired by Rhys's wanting to understand the character of Bertha Mason in Charlotte Brontë's *Jane Eyre*. Choose one of your favorite novels, and find a secondary character that is not well developed. Then write a short story about this character, filling out her history and giving her a stronger voice. In other words, write a story from this character's point of view.

- Antoinette enjoys very few moments of happiness in this novel. Find a passage in which she at least feels somewhat distracted from her sense of isolation, and write a song as if you were she, expressing your feelings about that moment.

- Antoinette mentions several dreams that she has. Pretend you are her analyst. What do you think her dreams mean? Do not worry about being accurate. Use your imagination, but try to base your conclusions on the details of Antoinette's life and what she must be feeling.

- Research slavery in the Caribbean. Then write a narrative as if you were a slave. Try to imagine what your life would be like. Choose a specific island, and decide the circumstances of your life. Are you someone who works in the fields, or someone who works in the house? Are you married? How old are you? From which African nation did you come?

- Research women and mental health. Are women's mental issues treated differently now than they were at the turn of the twentieth century? How do they differ? Then write a paper on how Antoinette might have been treated had she lived in the twenty-first century.

- The subject of voodoo is dealt with

in this novel. What is voodoo? Research this topic, and find out if it is still practiced today. Find out if there are still laws prohibiting the practice of voodoo. How do Christianity and voodoo conflict? Where is voodoo still practiced?

- Look into the phenomena referred to as the Sargasso Sea. What is it, and what causes it? Then write a paper on why you think Rhys used this as the title of her book. Explore the Sargasso Sea as a metaphor. How does this fit into the overall themes of the book?

Race Relations

Although not primary, the theme of race relations on the islands is woven throughout this story. The abolishment of slavery, although this happens before the story begins, affects the condition of life of Antoinette's family. Annette has no money to pay the freed slaves who used to work her family estate and this fact leads to her poverty. The anger between the white people and the black people, vestiges of the past, causes the destruction of Coulibri. At the other end of the spectrum, there is also the discussion of the mixed races, the children of white landowners and their female slaves. Antoinette's and Christophine's relationship demonstrates friendship between the races, one in which skin color might have affected the different ways both women were raised but also which shows how those differences can enhance their connection.

Point of View

Rhys uses multiple points of view in this novel. She begins with the voice of her female protagonist, Antoinette. At the start of the novel, Antoinette is a young girl, so the reader gains the child's perspective on the lives of the characters from a child's advantage. Rhys continues with this narrator through the first part of the story. In using the child as narrator, Rhys gives the reader a personal account of isolation as only a child can relate it. This device pulls the reader into the story on an emotional basis, setting the tone for the remaining parts of the story. She then switches, in the second part, to the point of view of Edward Rochester, the male protagonist. By this time, Antoinette is a newly wed young woman, and she and her surroundings are portrayed through Rochester's eyes. Rochester is not at home on the island. As a matter of fact, he feels extraordinarily alienated from everything about the island, from the colors of its vegetation to its local customs. By hearing the story from Rochester's point of view, the sense of isolation, one of the main themes of this novel, is further enhanced. Readers are also privy to Rochester's fears and doubts about Antoinette's stability, which is more objectively recorded as Antoinette slips deeper into her madness.

Antoinette regains the role of narrator in the middle of part 2. By this point, she is distraught over Rochester's inability to love her. Rhys must switch point of view at this stage because she wants the reader to witness the relationship of Antoinette and Christophine, who plot to regain Rochester's love of Antoinette. But when Antoinette loses all hope of regaining Rochester's love, the point of view once again switches back to Rochester. He has, at this point, become master of Antoinette, demanding that she leave her ancestral home and go to England.

In part 3, Rochester is completely missing from the story. So Rhys uses Grace Poole, a hired domestic, to fill in the gaps between the setting in the islands and the setting in England. Poole explains how she has been employed to take care of Antoinette who has become a rather wild and scary madwoman. After Poole's introduction to part 3, Antoinette once again gains control of the story as narrator. But her narration is distorted and unreliable. However, by this time, the story has unfolded as far as it is capable. The ending is inevitable. In using Antoinette's madness to close the story, Rhys leaves it to the imagination of the reader to fill in the blanks. Since she has based her story on Brontë's *Jane Eyre*, it can be assumed that Antoinette burns down the estate.

Setting

The story has several settings: Jamaica,

Dominica, and England in the middle of the nineteenth century. Although Rhys does not spend a lot of time describing any of these settings, the tone of her writing changes. While her characters are in the Caribbean, there is mention of sun and light, warmth, and perfumed scents. Her characters are often outdoors, and they confront other minor characters. Even though there are many challenges for each of the characters, there is also hope of positive outcomes. There is death, but there is also marriage. There are parties and swimming and good food, even though they are infrequent. The islands also represent both the positive and the negative of wilderness. There is the beauty of the wild over-growth of vegetation and the intensity of its colors. There is also the fear, the lack of safety, where law and order does not prevail. But once the characters move to England, readers confront dark, cold, sterile, and all but complete isolation.

Contrast and Similarity

Rhys uses contrast and similarity to construct not only her setting but also her characters. She compares the lives of the rich white people with the poor, the old white landowners with the new immigrant white families. She hints of the times when the white landowners used slaves and then shows the changes that occurred with the abolition of slavery. The conflict between the white people and the black people is demonstrated, but Rhys also mentions how many people are of mixed races, thus proving the sexual encounters between the two races. When Christophine uses voodoo in order to help Antoinette win back the affections of Rochester, Rhys has Rochester turn to the law, thus exposing the contrast between the beliefs of the local black population and those of white people's sense of rational order.

Similarities prevail throughout the story also. The major, and most obvious, one is that of Annette and Antoinette, who both suffer from a lack of love and understanding, which forces them to withdraw from reality. There is also a similarity between Mr. Mason, Annette's second husband, and Edward Rochester, Antoinette's husband. Both men do not understand their wives and appear to have little sense of their own emotions. Their attentions appear to be more on sex, money, and power. They also both had little respect for the black people who served them.

Dominica's Geography and Culture

Rhys was born and spent most of her childhood on the Caribbean island of Dominica. Most of Rhys's novel *Wide Sargasso Sea* is also set on this small island. Dominica is unique in that, because of its rugged landscape, much of the island has remained similar in appearance to the time that Christopher Columbus first saw it. Most of the island is covered in rain forest, receiving heavy rains each year. Dominica is the largest and most northerly of the Windward Island, with the Atlantic Ocean to its east and the Caribbean Sea to its west.

The culture of Dominica is unique. Before Columbus, the population was made up of Ciboneys people and Carib Indians. Most of them were killed when the European settlers arrived, beginning with the Spanish, followed by Great Britain and France. It was during the colonization of Dominica that slaves were brought to the islands to work on the massive sugar plantations. As a result of this combination of different cultures, Dominica's population contains characteristics that combine to make what is called Creole, or a mixing of cultures. These mixtures can be seen not only in the physical traits of its people but also in language, music, art, food, architecture, religion, dance, and dress. Many people of Dominica speak a patois, a mixture of

French with other languages of the area, in particular different African languages and Spanish.

Slavery in Dominica

Between 1518 and 1870, the transatlantic slave trade dramatically increased in the Caribbean. As sugarcane began to dominate the agricultural business of the Caribbean, Africans were shipped to the island in dramatically increasing numbers to add to and replace those who had come before them. In the early sixteenth century, an average of about two thousand slaves a year were shipped to the Caribbean from Africa. At its height, which occurred between 1811 and 1834, the slave trade accounted for about thirty-two thousand additional people being brought to the islands each year. Besides providing free labor, thus giving the white population a chance to gather immense wealth, the slave trade also created a black majority in the Caribbean islands.

Due to the increasing popularity and power of antislavery societies in Britain, a bill to abolish the slave trade passed both houses in 1807. It would not be until 1834 that slavery was abolished through the entire British Empire, which included the Caribbean islands. To replace the free slave labor, many landowners imported indentured workers from Asia and India. Although these people had legal contracts, they fared not much better than the African slaves they replaced. In the meantime, sugar prices fell due to competition from other countries, and a large population of freed slaves was unemployed. Many freed slaves formed their own villages, some of them squatting on abandoned lands and growing the same crops their former owners had raised in addition to new crops such as coconuts, rice, and bananas.

Dominican Economics

After slavery was abolished, white people found themselves in the minority and were divided along status lines based on wealth. Basically, there were rich whites and poor whites. The most elite of the rich whites were the plantation owners and former slave owners. Next came the white merchants, government officials, and professionals such as doctors. The poor whites included owners of small farms, laborers, and service people, such as policemen. No matter how much money a white person had, any white person of European descent gained a privileged position over black people. The black population consisted of free persons of color, freed slaves, and slaves. Economically, most black people during this time found themselves at the bottom of the list.

Education in Dominica

In the mid-nineteenth century, rich landowners more than likely would send their children abroad to be educated, whereas the more native whites sent their children to local private schools, most of them religious based. Black children received not much more than religious training, if anything at all. Some Caribbean island governments even made it illegal to teach blacks to read or write. Most local children who did attend school went there only until age sixteen.

The Sargasso Sea

The Sargasso Sea, the heart of the Bermuda Triangle, is a two-million-square-mile ellipse of deep-blue water adrift in the central North Atlantic. It was named after a Portuguese word for seaweed, *sargassum*, which is found in such abundance in this sea that Christopher Columbus feared his ships might become entangled in it. The waters in this floating sea are exceptionally clear and warm, but it unfortunately is relatively lifeless.

Ford Madox Ford

Ford Madox Ford played a substantial role both in Rhys's personal life and in her writing. He was an established writer and the influential founder of the *Transatlantic Review*, for which Ernest Hemingway was the editor. This publication helped to promote many young writers of the day. According to some accounts, Ford had at least twenty major affairs with prominent women and budding stars of his time. Rhys was just one of them. Ford also encouraged Rhys's writing and wrote the introduction to her first collection of short stories. He would break off his affair with her, but Rhys used the material of their affair for one of her later novels. Ford's most important literary works include *The Good Soldier*, a story of adultery and deceit.

Compare & Contrast

- **1850s:** In Dominica, black elected officials make up the majority of the general assembly. A few years later, whites push blacks out of power by demanding the British government to assign whites to seats in the assembly.

  1960s: Universal adult suffrage is granted to every citizen over twenty-one years of age in Dominica, swinging the power back to the people, regardless of land ownership or wealth.

  Today: Dominica enjoys full independence with a prime minister elected by the citizenry.

- **1850s:** White children of rich landowners are sent to Europe to be educated. White children of the less elite attend religious schools locally. Black children seldom learn to read or write.

  1960s: Construction of roads throughout the island allow rural children to attend schools more easily. The development of a public school system run by the government is also begun. Education is available to all races.

Today: Schools are available for all ages, from preschoolers through adults. However, there are no mandatory laws about attending school, and many children still do not attend, working full-time jobs instead.

- **1850s:** Although the land is relatively inexpensive (ten British shillings an acre), British laws demand that large tracts of land must be purchased. This keeps the land in the hands of the rich.

1960s: Former land laborers are given a chance to purchase their own land for the first time in Dominican recent history, thus allowing them to build better houses and afford education for their children.

Today: Dominica has the largest percentage of landowners per head of population than any other island in the Caribbean. This has provided the population with economic stability.

Critical Overview

The publication and wide critical acclaim of *Wide Sargasso Sea* returned Rhys to the spotlight. Her earlier popularity had faded, and her previous publications had gone out of print, leaving Rhys so lost to her public that most people thought she had died. *Wide Sargasso Sea*, having won two prestigious awards and being praised by literary critics as well as Rhys's general readers, caught everyone by surprise. After that, *Wide Sargasso Sea* remained popular. It has become, wrote a *Christian Science Monitor* critic, "Rhys's most famous novel." The novel portrays the plight of women, a theme that is recurrent in many of Rhys's works. The same *Christian Science Monitor* critic, for example, went on to state that all Rhys's female protagonists could be described in a similar way: "[T]he typical Jean Rhys heroine is a feminist's nightmare: a textbook illustration of what not to be." This view has not dissuaded feminist critics from exploring Rhys's work, however. Quite the contrary, even though Celia Marshik, writing for *Studies in the Novel*, claims that Rhys is "an insistent anti-feminist" who nonetheless has "created texts that feminists have claimed as their own."

Although many describe Rhys's female characters as weak and prone to acting out the role of victim, critic Jan Curtis states otherwise. Writing for *Critique: Studies in Contemporary Fiction*, Curtis believes that "[e]ach Rhys heroine struggles to heave herself out of the wide Sargasso sea found in every Rhys novel." Curtis goes on: "It is not until *Wide Sargasso Sea* that the Rhys heroine overcomes the Sargasso and discovers her strength in a fallen world of fractured consciousness and failed relationships by overcoming what [Wilson] Harris's narrator [in *Palace of the Peacock*] describes as the 'need in the world to provide a material nexus to bind the spirit of the universe.'"

It is hard to define Rhys, Marshik found. And rather than pigeonhole the author, Marshik concluded that Rhys "is a writer who seems to belong everywhere and nowhere." The reason for a resurgent interest in Rhys and her works, according to Tara Pepper, writing for *Newsweek*, is due in part to the fact that Rhys's "contemporaries were uneasy about her morally ambiguous, fractured characters and the seedy world she dwelt in, as well as wrote about." Pepper believes that Rhys's characters were too strange for the general public (especially British readers) to accept at a time when "inhabitants of former colonies were still considered culturally inferior." Today, Rhys's characters are better understood.

Wide Sargasso Sea, writes Dennis Porter for the *Massachusetts Review*, is "unlike her other novels with a contemporary setting," because it is based on another work of art (*Jane Eyre*). Although this influence strongly affected the way Rhys wrote her novel and, therefore, is not a "fully autonomous novel," it does, however, achieve "its purpose because it is a remarkable work of art in its own right." The story is written, states Porter, in a language that is lyrical, "a functional lyricism that incorporates both beauty and terror and simultaneously defines the limited consciousness of the two narrators."

Sources

Curtis, Jan, "The Secret of *Wide Sargasso Sea*," in *Critique: Studies in Contemporary Fiction*, Vol. XXXI, No. 3, Spring 1990, pp. 185–97.

"The Literary Life of Jean Rhys," in *Christian Science Monitor*, July 16, 1991.

Marshik, Celia, "Jean Rhys," in *Studies in the Novel*, Vol. 34, No. 1, pp. 116–18, Spring 2002.

Pepper, Tara, "Searching for a Home," in *Newsweek*, September 15, 2003, p. 58.

Porter, Dennis, "Of Heroines and Victims: Jean Rhys and *Jane Eyre*," in *Massachusetts Review*, Vol. XVII, No. 3, Autumn 1976, pp. 540–52.

Further Reading

Angier, Carole, *Jean Rhys: Life and Work*, Pubs Overstock, June 1991.

> In this biography and study, Angier links events in Rhys's life to characters and events in her stories and novels.

Bender, Todd K., ed., *Literary Impressionism in Jean Rhys, Ford Madox Ford, Joseph Conrad, and Charlotte Brontë*, Garland Publishing, 1997.

> After meeting with Joseph Conrad and then, twenty-five years later, with Jean Rhys, Ford Madox Ford is reported to have said that between these two writers, he saw the progression of modern literature toward impressionism. This text contains a collection of Ford's critical comments on impressionism, in particular the way in which Rhys's *Wide Sargasso Sea* forces readers to rethink Brontë's *Jane Eyre*.

Chesler, Phyllis, *Women and Madness*, Doubleday, 1972.

> Chesler provides a definitive study of the mental health of women who live in a patriarchal society. Her work revolutionized psychiatry,

providing new definitions of feminist therapy and demonstrating how women have often been controlled by conventional psychiatry.

Savory, Elaine, *Jean Rhys*, Cambridge University Press, 1998.

This is a critical study of Rhys's entire life's work, including her autobiography. Savory insists on looking at all of Rhys's work, keeping the author's Caribbean background in mind. This is an excellent study that keeps previous critical analyses on race, gender, class, and nationality in mind.

Williams, Eric, *From Columbus to Castro: The History of the Caribbean, 1492 to 1969*, Vintage Books, 1984.

Former prime minister of Trinidad and Tobago, Eric Williams outlines the common history of slavery in the Caribbean. In this book, Williams looks at the history of sugar and the free labor that provided wealth to a few and misery to over 30 million slaves.